A time of trains

DAVID PLOWDEN

A time of trains

W. W. Norton & Company   New York / London

The text of this book is composed in Simoncini Garamond.
Composition by Zimmering & Zinn, Inc.
Printed and bound in Great Britain by Balding & Mansell.
Book design by Hugh O'Neill.

First Edition

Library of Congress Cataloging-in-Publication Data
Plowden, David.
A time of trains.
1. Railroads—Pictorial works.   i. Title.
TF149.P56   1987   625.1'097   87-20351
ISBN 0-393-02499-7

ISBN 0-393-02499-7

W. W. Norton & Company, Inc., 500 Fifth Avenue, New York, N.Y. 10110
W. W. Norton & Company, Ltd., 37 Great Russell Street, London WC1B 3NU

1 2 3 4 5 6 7 8 9 0

to Glenn Hansen

A time of trains

There once was a time of trains vastly different from today; a time of romance and adventure, of great locomotives, of fast limiteds and steam whistles in the night. At train time one could feel the breath of the nation full of vigor, hot and panting; restive of spirit, poised at the depot. Then the train brought the world to the foot of Main Street, and no matter on which platform one stood it was possible to "hear America singing," to marvel at man's ingenious nature. Between trains the silent rails shone, reassuringly polished by countless wheels rolling the cargo of the nation and its people, promising there would be another train. And there always was: the local, a freight, Number 79, or the "Fast Mail" thundering past, burnishing the steel, keeping the promise, keeping the rust at bay. Then one could sit by the tracks and dream of other places, beyond the curve out of sight.

But almost no more. In these days of darkened stations and a countryside increasingly bereft of trains, where abandoned road beds are reverting to nature or being turned into hiking trails, it is hard to imagine that "Manifest Destiny" once rode the rails. There is little to remind us that America took shape along the railroads, and that for more than a century they were the "main street" of a growing country.

"Railroad iron is a magician's rod," wrote Emerson in 1836 at the dawn of the age of railroads. And so it proved to be. Railroad iron and the iron horse appeared at a providential moment in our history. In a vast and empty land they were as fundamental to its development as the frontier which they were so instrumental in subjugating. In this age of the automobile and the micro chip it is well to remember that the steam engine set in motion the process of successive technological innovation that has come to characterize all industrialized societies. From the moment the railroad builder and the locomotive upset the equilbrium of our pastoral existence nothing was ever the same again. If one has doubts remember that before the railroad Caesar and Andrew Jackson relied on the same method of land transport, the horse-drawn carriage—only the Romans had infinitely superior roads.

Although the heyday of the railroad and the steam locomotive was nearly past when I was growing up, railroads were still an integral part of the American scene. Passenger trains were the accepted and most available means of getting from one place to another. They went almost everywhere. In 1932, the year I was born, there were 73,981 communities in the United States, comprising just under 94 percent of the population, served by one or more railroads.

It wasn't until after World War II, and the advent of the Interstate Highway System in the 1950s and the jet plane that the railroads lost their preeminent position as the nation's common carrier. The statistics speak only too eloquently. In 1916, the year the railroad system in the United States reached its zenith, there were 254,000 miles of line, roughly a third of the world's total. By 1950 the figure was 236,999. Thirty five years later 90,000 more miles had been abandoned, and if we are to believe the prognosticators the system will have been pruned down to 100,000 by the year 2000.

In reality the American railroad system was vastly overbuilt and much of the mileage was redundant even before alternative means of transport were available. For years the railroads competed voraciously among themselves for traffic that seemed as plentiful as had the roaming herds of buffalo. However, once the competition in the form of trucks and barges began to siphon away the freight, and the populace turned to the automobile and the plane, many marginally profitable lines lost traffic and were abandoned. Even the mighty were not immune. The Rock Island is gone, the Milwaukee, the Lehigh Valley and the Lackawanna are gone too, dismembered or swallowed up by others in the recent spate of "mega-mergers." Gone, too, are such venerable institutions as the Baltimore & Ohio, The New York Central, the Pennsylvania, and its disastrous successor the Penn Central; the Great Northern and the Northern Pacific, the Nickel Plate, the Wabash, the Southern, the Frisco, the Texas & Pacific, the Erie and the New York, New Haven & Hartford, to name but a few. All were household words when I was growing up and seemed as secure as the Rock of Gibraltar.

Today, in spite of the fact that much of the fat has been trimmed away, the health of the system has not improved. In the past the railroad's stock-in-trade has always been the raw material and products of heavy industry. Nearly seventy-five percent of their traffic has traditionally been made up of such things as coal and iron ore, steel, automobile parts, pulp and paper and manufactured goods. But our economic base is no longer founded on manufacturing. Also the recent slump in the farm economy has meant a reduction in carloadings of agricultural products, another staple of the railroads. As a result the railroad industry has suffered a continual loss of traffic. Today it carries barely a third of the nation's freight and less than one half of one percent of all intercity passengers.

If the railroads survive as a viable part of America's transportation system, it will be in a very different form from the one depicted in this book. In the days of steam and great trains the industry required a disproportionally large work force and an enormous physical plant to operate. The steam engine, itself, was basically terribly inefficient and required a host of attendants to maintain it. The antediluvian work rules imposed by the unions did not help the railroads' position, either. Recently, however, much has been done to improve the situation, changing the face of railroading almost beyond recognition. Aside from the diesel, whose efficiency and labor saving economies proved to be the salvation of many a line, there have been other innovations such as Centralized Traffic Control, unit trains, pooling of motive power, automation of freight yards and track work, and computerization of many operations traditionally performed by the labor force. Even the caboose is disappearing from most freight trains as the size of the train crews is reduced. The most dramatic change, aside from the replacement of the steam locomotive, has been the almost complete demise of the passenger train from all but a few selected routes.

I have always loved trains. From the time I can remember the railroad has been my "leitmotif," appearing in one guise or another in all my work. My earliest recollection is of a locomotive in the night seen from the window of a lower berth. My first picture, made when I was eleven, was of a steam engine and for fifteen years thereafter I used the camera solely to photograph locomotives and trains. From the time I was a little boy I have spent as much time riding trains as possible. I sought out as many different railroads and trains as I could, never taking the same one twice if there was another choice. Over the years I have traveled hundreds of thousands of miles back and forth across the length and breadth of this continent. With the railroad as my tutor and my guide, the train window became the lens through which I formed my perception of America. Minor White, the great photographer and one of my mentors, said to me that unless I photographed "my damned engines and trains, and got them out of my system," I would never photograph anything else.

He was only partially correct. Over the nearly thirty years since he said that to me I went on to photograph many other things, but I have never gotten the railroads "out of my system." Somehow wherever I go I always find my way to the tracks and as long as there is a train going my way I'll be on it.

I am not sure why I love trains. Perhaps it is simply because the formative period of my life coincided with the twilight of steam and like many a boy I was overcome by the spell of locomotives. They were larger than life, the most impressive things in my experience. Wherever they appeared they commanded full attention. They were dangerous, magnificent, terrifying, exciting, immense, powerful and marvelous all at once. No one can convince me that they weren't the most compelling machines ever devised. Just watching one of those huge Central Vermont 700s getting under way with a heavy freight was all the proof I needed. Although I knew nothing about such things then, it wouldn't have surprised me to learn that no other machine occupied as important a place in our history, our music, our literature and folklore—our very consciousness, in fact.

As a child standing on the station platform at Putney, Vermont, watching the trains go by I had no idea, of course, that the steam engine on the morning local represented one of the quantum leaps in the history of mankind. Whenever I saw a pasture full of terrified heifers fleeing as the *White Mountain Express* hove into sight, I should have sensed that with the power of steam at his command man was certainly in the saddle. At the time I had no idea that the old Boston & Maine Pacific smoking up the landscape was a symbol of man's will to rise above nature. Nor was I concerned then, as I am now, with the social implications and destructive forces unleashed by an industrialized society that the locomotive also symbolized. None of these things entered by head. My love of railroads and locomotives was wonderfully uncomplicated. Life seemed as bright as a new penny.

By the time I started photographing in earnest most of the locomotives were already gone or were too far away. The few that were accessible became "actors" performing essentially the same roles as they might have anywhere. It was the part they played, not the individuals, that was important. That most were on the Canadian Pacific and the Central Vermont, which were close to home, or the Great Northern for whom I worked was immaterial. What mattered was that they were locomotives. A steam engine is a steam engine no matter where it is. It made no difference, either, on what side of the border they were. North American railroading is essentially the same whether north or south of the 49th parallel.

In retrospect it seems that I have made a career of being one step ahead of the wrecking ball. It was certainly true with the locomotives. I responded to the diesel as if awakened by the proverbial "fire bell in the night," and set forth on a mission to make a record of steam railroading before it vanished. I was barely in time. Many of the engines I photographed were during the last year, and at times the last week or even day, of their operation. Although the reason for taking to the field in the first place was obvious, once there it became my intention to give a feeling of what the era of steam railroading was like.

During that time I spent much time "behind the scenes," photographing the locomotive in its "lair," so to speak. The care and feeding of the locomotive required, not only a huge work force, but myriad specialized facilities, such as roundhouses, water plugs, coal docks, turntables and ash pits, all of which became hallmarks of the era of steam. By far the most interesting part of the terminal to me was the relationship of man and machine, the ritual of servicing the engines: cleaning the fires, taking coal and water, washing, "trimming" (lubricating the running gear), oiling 'round, and the like. All were performed in essentially the same time-honored fashion until the last fire was drawn on the last engine.

My favorite place was the roundhouse. It reminded me of a stable, and had all the same warmth and cozy sounds. No wonder the term "iron horse." The engines seemed alive, like breathing creatures, sighing and thumping away in the semi-dark. At rest they were infinitely approachable. It was possible to move among them, to walk along beside them and contemplate their wondrous mechanism. They were not unattended, but under the watchful eye of the hostler, who came by at regular intervals to tend the fires and make sure that there was enough water in their boilers, in much the same way as a stable boy would have watered the horses.

In 1960, when all steam locomotives were finally retired from active duty, a few were preserved and later resurrected to run on excursions for the benefit of the rail fan. In this role they seemed like veterans of long-ago campaigns who parade down "Main Street" on Memorial Day. Although these occasions were grand events they had little to do with the era of steam. Even so I picked up my cameras once again to record, not the event, but the locomotives. The engines themselves were the same.

The steam engine may have always been at center stage, but just as important has been the railroads' presence in the landscape. The railroads were the colonizers. They have been here a long time in American terms, long enough to have become part of what was once commonplace. Their presence no longer seems intrusive, as it must have been when the tracks cut the initial scar across the wilderness, and civilization with all its baggage followed in their wake. The faraway whistle in the night, the sight of a train in the distance rolling along under a cloud of steam, the depot; even the most prosaic things, like a water tank in the desert, a switch stand, telegraph lines striding along beside the tracks—and, of course, the tracks themselves—became symbols of progress, hated or revered as the case may be.

Just as the railroad became an integral part of the American culture, so now have the highways. Already the image of the open road stretching on across the western plains has replaced the one of the single track in the minds of most. The truck stop, the tractor trailer, the motel and almost anything to do with the automobile, have become part of America's symbolic iconography, as everything related to the railroads had been a generation ago.

The railroad's relationship to the towns and cities through which it passed and often nurtured, was as important as its relationship to land. This trackside environment, the railroad corridor, itself, became one of the most distinctly American places. Most of us know it in some way or another, if only from a train window. It is a place of grain elevators, coal tipples, warehouses, factories and mills, great and small, structures which have come to be particularly associated with the railroad, and which became among our most representative architecture. This is the backside view of America, for so many years the place where things happened and things were made. Often it was a smoky, grimy place, often hideously ugly, but always vital; a place which epitomized both the productive and inhumane side of man's nature. Today, however, it is more an archeological site, where the record of a multitude of endeavors survives in varying stages of usefulness and decay.

The railroad was a builder of its own towns, too, and not just those which sprang to life around water tanks, and the depots, but division points which grew up around engine terminals and freight yards, like Willmar and Cumberland, Thurmond and Megantic. These were spaced roughly every hundred miles along the line, the approximate distance a freight train could travel in an eight-hour day when the railroads were being built in the nineteenth century. All were basically the same place, composed of the same elements which gave then the unmistakable designation of "railroad towns."

In this day of the automobile it is hard to imagine the importance of the railroad depot in American life. For so long, it was a place where the experience with the world beyond Main Street began. In spite of their enormous architectural variety, the depots, like steam engines and railroad towns, were fundamentally the same no matter where they were. Those at Mount

Pleasant, Deposit, Canaan and Susquehanna, for example, despite their outward dissimilarity, are representative of the genre. Whatever its location, for over three generations, the depot was the focal point of many an American town. Such was usually not the case with the steamboat dock, and certainly not with the airport, both of which are located on the periphery, too far away to have an important role in the life of the town. The depot, on the other hand, was almost always located downtown, where quite literally and figuratively it occupied a central position in the affairs of the community. For the most part a town's economic base developed along the tracks and because virtually everything came and went by train, the station became the hub of activity. Even if there was no business to transact, or relative arriving from afar on the 4:20, the depot was definitely the place to be if one wanted to feel in touch with things. So it become a place to congregate, to kill time while "chewing the fat," much as the general store and barber shop had once been. More than anything, though, it was the place to be at train time.

This book is both a celebration and an elegy. It is about time—time past, and by inference, time present. The context of these photographs is of a generation or more ago, a time before diesels and Conrail, Amtrak and "X" companies. The "star" is, of course, the steam engine. The photographs have been garnered from literally thousands of my negatives taken over a span of thirty-five years, a great many of which had never been printed nor published before. Some of the locomotive pictures were taken long before I had any idea of becoming a full-time photographer, at a time when my only ambition was to become a railroader. During the process of sifting through all of the material for this book I was continually struck by the fact that although the photographs are the work of the same person, the earlier ones depict another generation's time. However, so much has changed since then that today it would be impossible to reconstruct an impression of what it was like. These early photographs are different in another way too. They are the product of a young, ingenuous eye, and represent another way of looking at the world which is very different from the way I see it today.

For those who do not know the time of trains and steam locomotives, it is hoped that the photographs may provide a catalyst for the imagination. For those who did know this time, I hope that in some measure this book will recall how important and wonderfully exciting it was.

My experiences with the railroads over the years have been many and varied; however, there is one that stands out above all the others as it best symbolizes railroading in the era of the steam engine. It was just before Christmas, 1955. At the time I was working for the Great Northern Railway in Willmar, Minnesota, a railroad town in the cornfields a hundred miles west of the Twin Cities. I had been assigned to the divisional office there and was given the rather grand but meaningless title of "Assistant to the Trainmaster." Being the youngest man there I usually worked the night shift. But this particular night was to be different from any other.

There was a terrible blizzard raging out on the high plains and all the trains from the west were running hours late. When I came on duty I discovered that Number Twenty-Eight, the *Fast Mail,* was running in two sections and that both had steam engines! Two of the four diesel units on First Number Twenty Eight had failed and a steam engine had been called upon to assist them. However, there were not enough diesels to go around and Second Number 28, was being pulled by one of the magnificent old mountain-type P-2s, the 2505.

The complete dieselization of America's railroads which began in earnest after World War II was only five years away by then. Relatively few lines still used steam engines and these were usually confined to specific areas or divisions. I was lucky enough to be assigned to the last stronghold of steam on the Great Northern where they were still quite frequently used on freight trains. However, there had not been a steam engine on a passenger train since I'd been at Willmar. Now, not one but two were headed my way.

I was damned if I was going to sit in the office that night. It might have been stretching the point a little. I knew that I would be expected to stay in town, but my duties were really quite irrelevant—at least I certainly hoped so right then. The yard master and dispatchers were old hands at coping with almost anything. The blizzard was really nothing in their eyes, so I reasoned my presence would be superfluous. I went into the chief dispatcher's office and told him that I was going to ride the engine on Second Number Twenty-Eight. He nodded his head without even looking up from his trainsheet. That was all I needed. I called up the roundhouse at Breneckridge and said, "Put a seat box on the 2505 for me."

There was never any question of which to ride. The engine on First Number Twenty-Eight was the 2588, a blue-ribbon engine in every way, but it was there to assist the diesels. The 2505 was doing the job alone. Moreover the P-2's were in a class by themselves. When they were built in 1923 they were the last word in passenger locomotive design. They had pulled the grand old *Oriental Limited* and the *Fast Mail* when it had been billed as "the fastest long-distance train in the world." One of them, the 2517, had been named the *Marathon*, after a run it had made in 1924 on one of the legendary "silk expresses," which raced across the continent at record speeds with trainloads of raw Japanese silk from the docks in Seattle to the mills of the eastern seaboard. The P-2's remained the Great Northern's premier engine until the 2588 and her sisters, the S-1s and the S-2s, replaced them. But tonight a P-2 was to be in the limelight once again.

There is nothing more lifeless than an unused piece of machinery, especially a locomotive without fire and steam. I'd often come upon engines like the 2505 languishing as "passenger protection" in an out of the way corner of a roundhouse waiting for a call. Try as I might I was never able to breathe life into my vision of one of them racing east towards St. Paul at the head of a trainload of silk. I had heard about how the switches were always "spiked" and how the railroad was given to the "silk expresses." But those were stories from another era, and the silent engines staring straight ahead out the windows of their roundhouse stalls kept their secrets and gave no more clues about their glorious exploits than the cold and mute bronze warriors lining the marbled corridors of a museum.

It was about two in the morning when I went outside to wait for First Number Twenty-Eight. I wasn't there for long before it appeared from the west like an apparition, all covered with snow and ice. As I watched the huge engine being serviced, I had second thoughts about my decision. The 2588 looked so magnificent I felt perhaps I should have ridden it after all. But before I had time to change my mind it was underway once more and gone; the only reminder that it had been there at all was its whistle growing fainter and fainter out east of town.

Then there was a lull, perhaps an hour or more of waiting, of going in and out of the dispatcher's office and downing cups of scalding black coffee before going back outside. It was bitter cold. The temperature was hovering somewhere around ten below, and the wind was howling off the plains straight out of the northwest. As anyone who has lived there knows, Minnesota winters are wicked. I'd seen conditions where the snow was packed so hard that it would derail a train, and I can remember nights spent with picks shovels and axes trying to open switches that had been frozen solid. I was on a branch line freight train once that got stalled in a drift, and all of us had to take refuge for the night in a nearby house.

I walked up and down the platform, watching my breath, hearing the squeak of the snow under my feet, stopping every so often to listen. My ears began to play tricks on me, I kept hearing what I thought was a whistle. It got later and later, the night colder. I was half frozen, but I wanted to be the first to hear it coming. I looked up at the sky; it was one of those absolutely crystalline nights when one can sense the universe expanding and has the feeling it is possible to look back to the very beginning of time. But down on the platform where I had been waiting for not the merest tick on the cosmic clock, it seemed as if time stood still.

Then, way out on the prairie, west of town, I heard it. There came the sound of a locomotive; a steam whistle, far out in the night. Ah, those Great Northern whistles. They were not deep like steamboats, not melodious, not high-pitched like those frigid whistles of the Central Vermont that I had grown up with. No, there was something about the Great Northern's whistles that was different from all the rest. They spoke as Jim Hill, the old "Empire Builder," himself, the first president of the Great Northern, might have, with a strident, no-nonsense, "get the hell out of my way, I'm coming through the snow, through the night," kind of authority. There has never been a sound to stir the soul like a locomotive whistle in the night, and that whistle over the cold frozen prairie spoke of the romance and adventure, of all that was railroading. Again and again and again it pealed, blowing, blowing for the crossings. Still far off, but coming closer and closer.

The activity began to pick up at the station. Several men went out and as I remember, lit two bonfires on either side of the track where the 2505 would stop to illuminate it while being serviced, as they had with the 2588. Once lit, they stood there waiting in the warmth, silhouetted against the flames. Others took up positions along the platform to be ready to inspect the train. But there were no passengers, for Second Twenty-Eight was purely a mail train tonight.

Close by now, not only the whistle, but the crackling exhaust of a locomotive in a hurry. As I listened, I heard the engineer shut off the steam. Then around the curve, west of the station, the headlight began to light the rails. And out of the night, out of the west, under a great cloud of steam, the 2505 appeared. It came charging by, like a gigantic iron messenger bringing dispatches from another realm and stopping panting directly in front of me, all steamy and hot. It had obviously done battle with the elements all night. Snow and ice were plastered from the top of the pilot beam right up to the headlight and the spokes of its immense driving wheels were sheathed in ice.

As I approached, I felt the heat of the great engine. It was magnificent, poised there like some giant creature catching its breath. Even at rest there was nothing quiescent about its nature. Laid out before me as plainly as blueprint was that most extraordinary of mechanisms, the running gear of a locomotive, that system of rods and cranks, valve gears and pistons organized with sublime precision and logic, which took steam and turned it into motion. The huge rods stretching along the drivers glistened in the light from the fires. Hot grease dripped from the crosshead guides and shone in little beads along the shaft of the piston. Little wisps of escaping steam rose from a dozen places, which only made the steam engine seem more restive. I could hear the air pumps thumping and the roaring inferno within the firebox. I looked up and saw the immense boiler. Suddenly the safety valve lifted with a deafening blast, and a column of superheated steam shot fifty feet or more straight up into the darkness, a reminder of the great forces contained within. I sensed the engine's impatience, its eagerness to be on its way, and felt all that pent-up energy could not be held in check much longer. There for a moment, standing under the stars, before the 2505, everything had been distilled to primal elements, just fire and ice; the engine full of Promethean vigor, breathing life into the frozen darkness.

The crew from the roundhouse that had come to service the engine set to work by the light of the fires. Two men began lubricating the immense crank pins on all four of the driving wheels with long sticks of hard green grease forcing it between the bearings with an oversize compressed air gun. The engineer climbed down from the cab, oil can in hand, and began that time honored ritual of "oiling 'round." Starting under the firebox he moved slowly and methodically along beside the rods and driving wheels pausing momentarily like a giant heron stalking his prey, thrusting the spout of the can here and there to place a drop of oil on a crucial spot. Down one side he went all the way up to the cylinders, then back the other out of sight. The fireman climbed up on top of the tender, pulled the water plug down and stood poised there with his foot on the spout while several thousand gallons of water poured into the tender. All along the platform the lanterns of the car-men bobbed up and down as they ducked in between and under the cars to see if all was well with the train.

The conductor, in a beige overcoat with the collar turned up against the cold, strode up and exchanged a few words with the engineer before he mounted the steps to the cab. The Great Northern was not one to waste a minute and within what seemed no time at all, the tasks were completed. I looked up and a great surge of excitement swept over me as I prepared to follow the engineer up the steps into the cab and take my place on the left-hand side behind the fireman on the seatbox I had ordered.

The image of that cab is something I shall never forget. It was a tiny, cramped space, with hardly room for three people, perched along as an afterthought behind the firebox of this long, lanky engine. It reeked of a heady combination of hot grease, steam, and fuel oil. Everything was covered with grime. It was dark except for the lights of the gauges and the flashing of the flames in the firebox. Behind us there was a heavy, thick rubber sheet that came down between the cab and the tender to close out the cold. The reason why engineers and firemen dressed the way they always did, in striped coveralls and cap, with a bandanna around the neck, and heavy gloves was immediately apparent. It was a matter of necessity, not style.

The engineer on the right, and the fireman on the left, sat facing the back of the firebox, the "backhead," which was an absolute plumber's nightmare. Upon it were laid out an indecipherable collection of gauges, valves, levers and pipes, which to the uninitiated seemed to have been arranged without any sort of logic. At the center, just above the floor plates, was the firebox door; all that kept the roaring "hell fire" at bay. Altogether, the cab was like a blacksmith shop. There was nothing at all refined or streamlined about the mechanics; nothing computerized. Steam engines didn't click and hum the way modern machines do, they thumped and banged away like a greatly oversized radiator. The locomotive itself was all brawn and muscle. In fact, despite a few important innovations, such as the power reverse, the air brake, and the mechanical stoker on coal burning engines, it was essentially a creation of the Industrial Revolution over a century earlier. There were no "aids to navigation" on a steam engine, save occasionally for a low water alarm, a speedometer and in a few instances, cab signals.

The locomotive cab was about the same size as the cockpit of an airliner, but it was almost like a Model "T" by comparison. In many ways the greatest difference between an airplane and a locomotive is the human side of the equation. It was up to two people, the engineer and fireman to run the engine, to keep it from blowing up, or from wrecking the train. There were no computers or flight controllers or radar to assist them. Of course, running a locomotive was hardly as complicated, nor did it require the training or skill that it does to fly a jet plane. Obviously the flight crew's responsibility is far more awesome, but they have myriad high-tech innovations on which to rely, whereas the engine crew, by comparison, ran the locomotive as if "by the seat of the pants," in the same way the old barnstorming pilots flew their planes.

There was another difference, too. It was possible without much effort to comprehend the rudiments of what the engineer and fireman did; to see how the locomotive, itself, worked. It was a beguilingly simply machine in spite of its enormous size. There was nothing covert about it, for its workings were completely accessible to the eye.

The engineer that night was a man named Brown. Brown was a taciturn thin fellow, probably in his late fifties or early sixties. He was the head of the local chapter of the Brotherhood of Locomotive Engineers and as such was regarded as a rather hostile figure by the people in the trainmaster's office. I myself had come to think of Brown as more a union man than railroad man. In fact I considered him as sort of an adversary, one to be viewed with suspicion because he sat on the opposite side of the bargaining table. So when I climbed up into the cab and saw him there, I wished it had been someone else. But it was Brown who greeted me, with no more than a grunt to acknowledge the fact that I would be riding with him. Engineers and firemen, most train crews, as a rule, hated it when trainmasters, especially trainmasters' assistants, rode with them. It meant that they had to follow the rule book exactly, so I'm sure that Brown wished I wasn't in the cab that night.

However, as far as I was concerned, I wasn't there in my official capacity. I was there to ride the 2505. I would have liked to have told Brown that; not to worry, to forget me, that it was his engine and to run it as he pleased.

I don't remember the name of the fireman, yet I was sitting with my head not more than a foot from the back of his neck the entire way to St. Paul. In spite of the fact that he remained in his seat most of the trip we hardly spoke at all, so great was the noise in the cab. Although most steam locomotives burn coal, the 2505 was an oil burner like virtually all of the Great Northerns, so the fireman's job was hardly as taxing as it would have been a generation before when he might have had to shovel as much as ten or even twenty tons of coal into the firebox during a run. His task was similar to the fireman's on a stoker fired coal burner, which was accomplished, not by back breaking effort, but manipulating various valves and levers. Nonetheless the fireman's job required no small amount of skill. He had to anticipate the needs of the engineer and fire the engine accordingly, always making sure there was enough steam without wasting water or fuel.

It was Brown I remember. He went to work at once settling himself in for the run, ignoring us completely. The window on his side had been frozen shut by hundreds of miles of blowing snow. He found a "fusee" and lit it to melt the ice so that it could be opened. When it came unstuck he kept slamming it back and forth angrily, swearing and spitting tobacco juice; complaining perhaps because he wished this were a diesel tonight. Brown was a passenger man used to the comforts of a diesel's cab. After he was satisfied with the window, he lifted the lid of his seat box and took out a big wad of cotton waste—the ubiquitous cleaning material of the steam era, mill ends, bits and shards of cloth and thread from the cotton mills—and began to wipe off the gauges, the throttle and all the other valves and levers he was going to use. As Brown went round polishing and cleaning, I thought of all the other engineers whose hands had grasped those levers and remember being struck with how beautifully worn and smooth the levers looked.

The signal for the brake test came and suddenly the cab was filled with the deafening sound of the air being drawn off the brake line. Brown turned and thrust his head out of the window and looked back along the train to watch for the signal to release the air. It came almost immediately and once again the hiss of escaping air filled the cab as Brown released the brakes. Then he turned to the task at hand. Almost instinctively he leaned forward and his right hand reached for the power reverse lever and pushed it all the way down into the corner. This lever, which controls the valve gear, determines not only the direction of the motion—forward or reverse—but at what point during the stroke of the piston steam will be cut off to the cylinders. Knowing just how to do this is one of the fine points of running a locomotive. When starting an engine, or when full power is needed, steam is admitted to the cylinder for the full length of the piston stroke. Once it is underway, however, the engineer hooks up the lever, notch by notch, thus cutting off the steam before the stroke is completed so that the steam's own expansion while cooling drives the piston to the end of its stroke. Using steam, in this manner, is generally the most economical way of working a locomotive.

A moment later Brown's left hand reached out for the throttle. He pulled it back gently a notch or two and the 2505 took a tremendous breath and started to move. I don't remember exactly how many cars we had, perhaps fourteen or fifteen. It was a heavy train though and the engine struggled mightily to get us underway. Brown kept her steady, knowing how much steam to use and never once let the drivers slip. I put my head out of the window and looked up at the towering column of steam and smoke disappearing into the blackness above the engine. The thundering cadence grew louder, drowning out all else, as Brown coaxed the 2505 onward. I felt goose pimples rising on the back of my neck. I looked down from the window and by the light of the street lamps saw the driving rods moving up and down and back and forth, making the drivers roll. Faster and faster now with each revolution as Brown and the 2505 took Second Number Twenty-Eight out of town. As I listened the sound of the exhaust assumed a greater sense of urgency as the speed began to increase. This was the *Fast Mail* after all, "the fastest long-distance train in the world." We were hours late, and as they had with the "silk expresses," the Great Northern had given us the railroad. There was nothing in our way and Brown knew it.

Once the initial task of getting underway had been accomplished Brown settled back a little in his seat. But his left hand was still on the throttle. He kept pulling it back further and further until I thought he was going to pull it right through the roof of the cab. In spite of the cold he had left his window wide open enough to hear the exhaust, to listen to the sound of the engine. As I watched him I realized, that like most of the other old-timers, Brown never paid the slightest attention to the gauges that he had wiped so carefully.

He reminded me of Johnson, another engineer I had often ridden with, who when I asked him why he always kept his head out of the window and never looked at any of the dials on the backhead, replied, "I don't have to. I listen to the exhaust. It tells me everything. Just like playing the piano by ear."

Suddenly Brown's hand moved from the throttle to the whistle cord and over the din rose the voice of the 2505, proclaiming to all that this was Second Number Twenty-Eight, the *Fast Mail* coming through. Brown played the whistle for all it was worth, made it moan and wail and shout as if to rouse the sleepers from their beds and bring them to their windows to celebrate the event. He was unrelenting. He held down the whistle cord through every little town—two long, one short and one more long wavering call—holding on to the last, drawing it out, letting it slowly trail off until he finally let it go. Over and over again the whistle blew, yet, as I remember, nobody was there to witness our passage. The only soul I saw out there was a man in a snow plow clearing the highway. But I knew people must be awake, the Middle

West gets up early. Here and there lights were beginning to turn on in the farmhouses and in windows along the back streets.

Now the 2505 began to lope. Every engine's motion was as different and distinctive as a particular fingerprint. Some locomotives were real "liver splitters," like bucking broncos, so rough you had to hold on for dear life for fear of being thrown out of the cab. Others were solid and rode like a Pullman. The 2505 had a sort of rolling gait; a slight sideways motion, almost as if it had a trace of a limp. It was an old engine, but like all those on the Great Northern, it was beautifully maintained, a fact which I tried to keep in mind as the speed increased.

All the while Brown had not spoken a word to either of us. He was sitting there hunkered down on his seat, one arm hung over the throttle, silently tending to his business, completely absorbed, one with his engine, oblivious to anything else. By now he had the 2505 working full out. I kept my eye on the speedometer, watching the needle climb. There was a 79 mile an hour speed limit for passenger trains on the Great Northern, and the P-2s were supposed to be restricted to 70 miles an hour, but I don't think anyone was terribly concerned about speed limits that night, and Brown had obviously decided to ignore my "official" presence.

As I watched, the needle reached 80, then a little later 85. The next time I looked over it was at nearly 90. As we approached the outskirts of Litchfield about 25 miles east of Willmar, it had reached 92, and there it stood, hovering on one side or the other of 90 miles an hour—a mile in 40 seconds—20 miles an hour more than the 2505 was designed to run. I knew that speedometers on steam locomotives were notoriously inaccurate, in fact many had none at all, so we might have been only doing 85, but from the way the engine felt, we could have as easily been doing a hundred. Whatever the actual speed, from the way it felt inside the cab it might as well have been "warp speed." The old engine was shaking so much that I had to hold onto the window sill to keep from falling off the seat box. The noise was incredible. The roar of the fire, which was now white hot, the cacophony of clanging and crashing of metal was deafening. The sense of being propelled forward was so exhilarating that it felt as if we were no longer connected to the earth. I kept looking at the speedometer and at Brown beyond, just to keep my bearings. Neither moved.

Howling through Litchfield now at 92 miles an hour, the whistle shrieking, the roar of the exhaust absolutely deafening as the town closed in around us and the sounds of the engine reverberated back and forth between the buildings.

In spite of the cold I leaned out the window as far as I dared to be closer to it all; to feel the wind in my face, to see the headlight piercing the night ahead and the crossing gates coming down on the empty streets, to see the rolling drivers, the rods racing in a blur and was completely swept along with the engine.

Litchfield disappeared in a flash. Its lights were already like those of a far off galaxy receding behind us as we plunged on into the night. Brown, implacable old Brown, was carrying the banner for all of his kind. On and on we raced, unrelentingly devouring the miles.

Town after town in succession across the map, though God knows it might have been across the heavens—Darwin, Cokato, Howard Lake, Waverly, Montrose, Delano. Flat out now, racing hellbent for St. Paul, trying to take a bite out of time.

To all railroaders of that era the concept of being "on time" was practically genetic. When a train was late it was understood that every effort would be made to make up as much time as possible before reaching the next terminal. It was a sort of wager, or relay race, in which each train crew passed the baton, so to speak, onto the next, who would in turn do their best to make up even more time. This preoccupation with being "on time" was not solely a matter of not inconveniencing the traveling public or company policy, but was equally a matter of pride on the part of the engine crews. Many an engineer's reputation rested upon his ability to shave a few minutes off the clock. Alas, far too many wrecks have been caused for the sake of being "on time." Railroad folklore is replete with tales of brave engineers like Casey Jones and the man at the throttle of "Old 97," fast runners who pushed their luck too far and came to grief.

The way Brown was "scorching the ballast" tonight I felt we might leave the rails at any moment. We roared down the Great Northern's mainline like the proverbial "bat out of Hell"; it certainly seemed as if the old 2505 was going faster than the speed of light. The irony was that we were already so late that the few minutes we might gain wouldn't matter one way or the other. But Brown had a tradition to uphold.

As we streaked onward I wondered if the 2505 was capable of sustaining such speed? Would it still hold together?

After all, it was 32 years old—old for a machine—and until it had been fired up tonight, it had been sitting out of service in some far corner of the roundhouse in Minot for who knows how long. What about metal fatigue? Would the old rivets begin to pop, or an axle break, or one of the rods shear off and come flailing back into the cab? Would the vibration cause a pipe to burst and fill the cab with scalding steam? Brown, too, as I noticed from the level of the water in the glass was "trading water for steam," as they say, running the engine on "blue steam," keeping as little water in the boiler as possible. I just hoped there was enough to keep the crownsheet on top of the firebox covered, otherwise as I knew full well the staybolts would melt and the engine explode. Then there were those 55 and 60 mile an hour curves I knew were coming soon. Would Brown slow down in time? I looked at him again. He seemed as reassuringly dispassionate as ever. If those disquieting thoughts had crossed his mind they were obviously of little concern to him. He was sitting there implacably, stretching the 2505 to the limits, making it reach to even greater heights, asking that wonderful machine to pour forth everything it had. Suddenly, Brown was no longer an adversary, the local representative of the Brotherhood. He was magnificent, a real engineer, this union man.

I kept having the feeling that somehow I shouldn't really be here, that I hadn't yet earned the right to have such an adventure. But I had my gold pocket watch and my pass which said "good on freight trains and locomotives," and I was, after all, here tonight officially as a representative of the management of the Great Northern. I was on their payroll. I had been told to go out and learn railroading, ride trains and engines. But in the bottom of my heart I knew that this was just rationale—a ruse. I should have been back in the office just in case John Boyd, the trainmaster, might have called up to ask me how things were. It was too late to bother with that now. The hell with it. Nothing would have prevented me from taking this ride.

And then suddenly without warning it was there in the eastern sky. Almost imperceptible at first, but gaining force, light began to come and with it the terrible realization that the run was nearly over. I turned quickly away and looked in the other direction, but when I turned back it was unmistakably morning. The world was finite, defined once more and all the more diminished, I felt, for being visible. Out on the prairie in the night, all the way to the outskirts of Minneapolis, the world was ours. The night, the stars, the 2505, the whistle and Brown were all that mattered. We were the *Fast Mail*, the *Midnight Special*, and all those night trains whose whistle stirred the imaginations of those who heard its incantations. But with the dawn came the suburbs awakening, people filling the streets, going to work, starting their routine. I wondered as they waited in their cars for us to pass whether any were aware of the significance of the 2505's run, or whether the train was just something in their way. It's hard to believe that anybody would be so blasé not to have been stirred by the sight of a locomotive streaking past at daybreak on a wintry morn under a full head of steam. But no matter what they may have thought, to me all of them were interlopers. This was our dawn, not their's. We'd earned it. We'd been up all night, racing against the clock, with the Christmas mail.

Then, as if awakened from a dream, we were surrounded by the city; threading our way through Minneapolis and into the cavernous trainshed. We were there a long time as mountains of mail were unloaded, but my mind and body had not yet adjusted to the fact that we were standing still. I was still somewhere out there on the prairie before dawn, not in this alien place. Had we raced all night to catch up with time, our time again?

Once stopped, the heat in the cab was almost stifling despite the fact that the windows on both sides were wide open. The fireman and I leaned out ours and made small talk, but Brown, leaning out of the window on the other side of the cab kept whatever his thoughts were to himself. While we waited I thought of all the other times I had been in a locomotive cab and realized how familiar this place was to me. I was struck too with the realization that the 2505 was nearly at the end of its journey while mine was just beginning. I had come in on the twilight of an era that was almost at an end. Soon there would be no more locomotives to ride. The diesels had taken command and it was just a matter of mopping up a few pockets of resistance, just a matter of time before Brown would be back on the diesels.

Finally the mail was unloaded and we started across the great stone bridge over the Mississippi east of the station. The 2505 began to thunder as it worked hard to get the heavy train started one more time. The effort was so great I felt the drivers might begin to slip; that it would falter, but then I remembered that Brown's steadying hand was there. The sun was up now and the light caught the boiler jacket, all black and shiny. Now for the first time the power of the engine was in full view. I looked down and watched the intricate motion of rods and the wheels all orchestrated in unison to drive the engine onward. As we crossed the bridge I turned and looked back at the long line of mail cars following behind us under a rolling, boiling cloud of steam and smoke. We labored on past the factories and grain elevators along the river and by the time we reached the yard at Minneapolis Junction, the 2505 had begun to hit its stride again. But it was a different stride. The goal was not speed but power to lift the heavy train up the hill that separates the Twin Cities and it seemed now as if the 2505 was giving Brown every last ounce of energy it had to surmount the obstacle. This was the final effort and the old engine stormed its way up the grade with a thundering voice that filled the sky and brought passers-by to a standstill. Once again I felt goose pimples on the back of my neck. A group of track workers cleaning switches stopped and looked up, I felt, to cheer us on. Someone leaned out of a doorway and raised an arm in salute. Further down the line some children on their way to school stopped to wave. Because I had been through the night on the 2505 and because I was a railroader, I felt I had earned the right to wave back. But you always have to be a little blasé when you wave from the cab of an engine. After all, you are looking down at ordinary people.

All at once, something was different. The laboring exhaust became easier. We had reached the top of the grade. It was all downhill now. I could almost feel the 2505 beginning to relax. But I could not; with all my heart I was trying to soak up those mesmerizing locomotive sounds and smells; absorb as much as I could before it was over. I wanted to be back on the platform at Willmar again, about to mount the steps to the cab, or howling through Litchfield again, anywhere but here. It had all gone so fast. Brown closed the throttle, the engine began to drift. A moment later the hiss of air from the brake valve confirmed that we were nearly there. Slowly we picked our way through the switches and onto the tracks leading to the station. And with its bell tolling, the 2505 steamed into St. Paul.

Directly across the platform from where we came to a stop was a pair of diesels which had just arrived on the *Northwestern Limited* from Chicago. The engineer was already down on the platform talking to the conductor. No sooner had we come to a halt than Brown suddenly sprang to life. He uncoiled himself from the crouched position he had been sitting in most of the night—he was a tall man, I realized then—and without a word to me or the fireman he climbed down out of the cab. The moment he hit the ground he turned and rushed over to the engineer of the Chicago train and grabbing him by the straps of his overalls, he exclaimed pointing to the 2505, "Look what I brought into St. Paul this morning!"

By then I had come down from the engine myself. Brown wheeled around and threw his arm around my shoulder and said, "Boy, can that old girl run. Boy, did we get her worked up tonight. My God, what a run we had, eh? God, what a run!"

Taciturn old Brown, the union man. Every time I saw him after that, his eyes would light up and he'd say, "Boy, do you remember that run we made? Remember that night? Boy, could she run! Will you ever forget it?"

That was, as far as I know, the last run of a steam engine on a passenger train on the Great Northern.

I often thought about Brown. There was no mandatory retirement age for engineers then, so he probably had a good ten years or more to go before he took his pension. Perhaps in that time, the night on the 2505 would have taken on a different perspective, somewhat diluted by the routine of work. He stayed and I left. Because I did, I carried with me all the events of my short career on the railroad preserved in amber, so to speak.

Almost all the tangibles of that time are gone. The 2505 was scrapped years ago, melted down, reused and recycled into iceboxes or cars or gun barrels several times over. The Great Northern, the Empire Builder's railroad itself, has become part of the Burlington Northern system. St. Paul Union Station is no longer a station. The *Fast Mail* and all the passenger trains on the Willmar division are gone, too.

The 2588 survived. It is preserved like a stuffed bison behind a chainlink fence next to the station at Havre, Montana. The 2505 fared better, I believe. It has gone to Valhalla.

Canadian Pacific Railway. Locomotive in roundhouse, St. Luc engine terminal, Montreal, Quebec.

Canadian Pacific Railway. Locomotives in roundhouse, the Glen engine terminal,
Montreal, Quebec.

Canadian Pacific Railway, 2-8-2 type locomotive #5145,
Montreal, Quebec.

Canadian Pacific Railway. Driving wheels and running gear of locomotive #5145, Montreal, Quebec.

Canadian Pacific Railway 2-8-2 type locomotive #5145, Montreal, Quebec.

Canadian Pacific Railway, The Glen engine terminal, Montreal, Quebec.

Canadian Pacific Railway, The Glen engine terminal, Montreal, Quebec.

Canadian Pacific Railway, The Glen engine terminal, Montreal, Quebec.

Canadian Pacific Railway, The Glen engine terminal, Montreal, Quebec.

Canadian Pacific Railway. Conductor handing orders to engineer, Windsor Station, Montreal, Quebec.

Canadian Pacific Railway. Trains departing Windsor Station, Montreal, Quebec.

Canadian Pacific Railway. Locomotive #2408 departing Vaudreuil, Quebec.

Reading Company 4-8-4 type locomotives 2124 and 2100 doubleheading train,
Port Clinton, Pennsylvania.

Fireman's side of Canadian Pacific Railway locomotive #5107.

Locomotive engineer.

Reading Company. 4-8-4 type locomotives #2100 and 2102 doubleheading train at Port Clinton, Pennsylvania.

Reading Company. 4-8-4 type locomotives #2124 and 2100 doubleheading train near Port Clinton, Pennsylvania.

The Sciotoville Bridge, Chesapeake & Ohio Railway, Ohio River, Sciotoville, Ohio.

The Tunkhannock Viaduct, Lackawanna Railroad, Nicholson, Pennsylvania.

Chicago & Northwestern Railroad tracks west of Mechanicsville, Iowa.

Great Northern Railway. Extra 3377 east near Atwater, Minnesota.

Great Northern Railway. Extra 3387 east leaving Willmar, Minnesota.

Great Northern Railway. Extra 3387 east near Willmar, Minnesota.

Great Northern Railway. Extra 3383 east near Kandiyohi, Minnesota.

Great Northern Railway. Extra 3377 east near Atwater, Minnesota.

Great Northern Railway. Westbound freight train west of Havre, Montana.

Looking west along Chicago, Milwaukee, St. Paul & Pacific Railroad Tracks near Scenic, South Dakota.

Great Northern Railway right-of-way, looking west from Spotted Tail, Montana.

Crane beside Southern Pacific Railroad spur track near Cortaro, Arizona.

Chicago, Milwaukee, St. Paul & Pacific Railroad yard and engine terminal, Bozeman, Montana.

Coal tipple on Norfolk & Western Railway mine spur near Slab Fork, West Virginia.

Denver & Rio Grande Western Railroad. Freight train climbing grade to Cumbres Pass, Colorado.

Denver & Rio Grande Western Railroad. Engineer oiling 2-8-2 type #494 at Cumbres, Colorado.

Fireman watering Pennsylvania Railroad locomotive #5244. Union Transportation Company,
Wrightstown, New Jersey.

Sydney & Louisburg Railway, Glace Bay, Nova Scotia.

Boston & Maine Railroad train #3808 at Claremont Junction, New Hampshire.

Sydney & Louisburg Railway mixed train at Louisburg, Nova Scotia.

Southern Pacific/Western Pacific Railroad depot, Beowawe, Nevada.

Buildings beside Chicago & Northwestern Railway tracks, Ironwood, Michigan.

West Pawlet, Vermont as seen from Deleware & Hudson Railroad bridge.

Clinton, Wisconsin as seen from Chicago & Northwestern Railway depot.

Chesapeake & Ohio Railway, Thurmond, West Virginia.

Chesapeake & Ohio Railway, Thurmond, West Virginia.

Cumberland, Maryland as seen from Baltimore & Ohio Railroad tracks.

Cumberland, Maryland as seen from Baltimore & Ohio Railroad tracks.

Keystone, West Virginia as seen from Norfolk & Western Railway main line.

Norfolk & Western Railway yard, Welch, West Virginia.

Buffalo, New York.

Milwaukee Road right of way, Milwaukee, Wisconsin.

Central Railroad of New Jersey bridge over Lehigh Valley Railroad, Lehighton, Pennsylvania.

Penn-Central Railroad yards, Chicago, Illinois.

Chesapeake & Ohio Railway yard, Presque Isle, Ohio.

Delaware & Hudson Railway. "FA" tower and yard, Oneonta, New York.

Switchman pulling pin, Delaware & Hudson Railroad, Mechanicville, New York.

Track worker, Penn-Central Railroad, Altoona, Pennsylvania.

Brakeman coupling cars, Delaware & Hudson Railroad, Whitehall, New York.

Rail laying crew, Penn-Central Railroad, near Cresson, Pennsylvania.

Central Railroad of New Jersey, signal bridges and tracks, Jersey City passenger terminal.

View of Pittsburgh, Pennsylvania as seen from Pittsburgh & Lake Erie Railroad right of way.

Elgin, Joliet & Eastern Railway yard and United States Steel Company coke plant, Gary, Indiana.

*View of steel mills, Braddock, Pennsylvania as seen from Pittsburgh & Lake Erie Railroad
right of way.*

LTV Corporation steel mill, East Chicago, Indiana.

United States Steel Corporation Mintac taconite plant, and Duluth, Missabe & Iron Range Railway yard, Virginia, Minnesota.

Steel Mill along Indiana Harbor Canal, East Chicago, Indiana.

Sydney & Louisburg Railway engine terminal, Sydney, Nova Scotia.

Canadian Pacific Railway, The Glen engine terminal, Montreal, Quebec.

Canadian Pacific Railway, The Glen engine terminal, Montreal, Quebec.

Canadian National Railways. Locomotive backing out of roundhouse, Hamilton, Ontario.

Canadian National Railways 4-8-4 type locomotive #6218.

Canadian Pacific Railway. Engineer oiling locomotive, the Glen engine terminal,
Montreal, Quebec.

Canadian Pacific Railway. Man making repairs to locomotive smokebox, St. Luc engine terminal, Montreal, Quebec.

Canadian National Railways. Coal Docks, Hamilton, Ontario.

Central Vermont Railway 2-10-4 type locomotive #707, White River Junction, Vermont.

Canadian Pacific Railway. Locomotive taking coal, Brownville Junction, Maine.

Quebec Central Railway. Locomotive taking water, Vallee Junction, Quebec.

Central Vermont Railway. Cleaning fires, White River Junction, Vermont.

Denver & Rio Grande Western Railroad. Locomotive taking sand, Chama, New Mexico.

Canadian Pacific Railway. Washing locomotive, McAdam, New Brunswick.

Canadian Pacific Railway. Washing locomotive, McAdam, New Brunswick.

Canadian National Railways 4-8-4 type locomotive #6218 detail.

Duluth, Missabi & Iron Range Railway 2-8-8-4 type locomotive #220, Two Harbors, Minnesota.

Canadian Pacific Railway. 2-8-2 type locomotive #5107, Megantic, Quebec.

Canadian Pacific Railway yard, Megantic, Quebec.

Canadian Pacific Railway. Local freight train east of Cookshire, Quebec.

Quebec Central Railway. Freight train near Ste. Marie, Quebec.

Quebec Central Railway, North Hatley, Quebec.

Central Vermont Railway, Brattleboro, Vermont.

Great Northern Railway Extra 3375 east, Kandiyohi, Minnesota.

Unit coal train, Illinois Central Gulf Railroad, Ashkum, Illinois.

Grain elevators along former Illinois Central Railroad, Aurelia, Iowa.

Canadian Pacific Railway, Harvey, New Brunswick.

Southern Pacific/Western Pacific Railroad depot, Beowawe, Nevada.

Lehigh Valley Railroad depot, South Plainfield, New Jersey.

Erie Railroad station, Susquehanna, Pennsylvania.

Erie Railroad depot, Deposit, New York.

Ann Arbor Railroad depot, Mt. Pleasant, Michigan.

New York, New Haven & Hartford Railroad depot, Canaan, Connecticut.

Central Railroad of New Jersey depot, Wilkes-Barre, Pennsylvania.

Lehigh Valley Railroad depot, Wilkes-Barre, Pennsylvania.

Erie Railroad station, Susquehanna, Pennsylvania.

New York Central Railroad Station, St. Thomas, Ontario.

Trainshed, Central Vermont Railway station, St. Albans, Vermont.

Central Railroad of New Jersey City Passenger Terminal, Jersey City, New Jersey.

Erie-Lackawanna Railroad. Westbound "Phoebe Snow" at Scranton, Pennsylvania.

Reading Railroad. Waiting room Outer Station, Reading, Pennsylvania.

Waiting room, New York, New Haven & Hartford Railroad depot, Canaan, Connecticut.

Waiting room Canadian Pacific Railway station, St. Johnsbury, Vermont.

Scale, Reading Company Outer Station, Reading, Pennsylvania.

R.H. Birkhead, agent Missouri-Kansas-Texas Railroad, Frederick, Oklahoma.

Chicago & Eastern Illinois Railroad depot, Princeton, Indiana.

Office, Erie Railroad depot, Thompson, Pennsylvania.

Ticket office bay window Lehigh Valley Railroad depot, Rochester Junction, New York.

Yard office Baltimore & Ohio Railroad, East Salamanca, New York.

Waiting for arrival of the "Phoebe Snow," Erie-Lackawanna Railroad depot, Waverly, New York.

Loading mail onto Baltimore & Ohio Railroad train #11, Piedmont, West Virginia.

James White, conductor Lehigh Valley Railroad train #9, the "Black Diamond,"
Wilkes-Barre, Pennsylvania.

Baggageman, Erie-Lackawanna Railroad train #21, Susquehanna, Pennsylvania.

"19" Train orders, Baltimore & Ohio Railroad, Harpers Ferry, West Virginia.

Freight train, Southern Railway Orange, Virginia.

Main Street, Nevada, Ohio as seen from Pennsylvania Railroad right-of-way.

Chicago, Milwaukee, St. Paul & Pacific Railroad depot and grain elevators, Parkston, South Dakota.

Union Pacific Railroad depot and grain elevators, Cheyenne Wells, Colorado.

Soo Line depot, Martin, North Dakota.

*Trackside buildings beside Atchinson, Topeka & Santa Fe Railroad right of way,
Wagon Mound, New Mexico.*

Carter, Montana.

Grain Elevators beside Northern Pacific Railway, Golden Valley, North Dakota.

Cattle loading chute, Nevada Northern Railway, Currie, Nevada.

Fort Worth & Denver City Railway [Burlington Lines] right of way near Perico, Texas.

Atchinson, Topeka & Santa Fe freight train and grain elevator, Sanderson, Kansas.

Grain elevator and cemetery beside Illinois Railroad Terminal tracks.
Union, Logan County, Illinois.

Colorado & Southern Railway [Burlington Lines] tracks, Grenville, New Mexico.

Grain Elevators beside Northern Pacific Railway tracks, Sykeston, North Dakota.

Northern Pacific Railway freight train near Elliston, Montana.

Northern Pacific Railway freight train near Elliston, Montana.